W9-CXK-653

UGLY DUCKLING PRESSE :: DOSSIER

First Edition, First Printing 2011
Printed in the USA

Library of Congress Cataloging-in-Publication Data

Magi, Jill.
  Slot / by Jill Magi.
       p. cm.
  ISBN 978-1-933254-87-6 (pbk. : alk. paper)
  I. Title.
  PS3613.A3448M34 2012
  811'.6--dc23

                        2011035063

Distributed to the trade by
Small Press Distribution
www.spdbooks.org

Available directly from UDP and through our partner bookstores:
www.uglyducklingpresse.org/orders
www.uglyducklingpresse.org/bookstores

Ugly Duckling Presse
The Old American Can Factory
232 Third Street #E-002
Brooklyn, NY 11215

www.uglyducklingpresse.org

SLOT

Jill Magi

for joanna –
with deep appreciation
for your work !

warmly,

Jill
Oct 2011
@ LMCC

SLOT

I follow museum workers down hallways until they slip into the walls,
out of my quiet, freedom, thoughts, and a little sad.

For an afternoon, rooms to learn turn into spirals and atriums. Business offices
are invisible, away in a wing. They carry keys as I remain—

Dear J.,
Meet me at open pillars.

An explanation walks past, adjusts her glasses as I, my posture.

Relief at the entrance, reverent coat-check, the hanging clang of metal against
racks.

Are you ready-vocal, able-bodied, or flagged and wheeled?

I wait for you, feeling hallway, feeling marble thought carved and well said.
A bench at the fountain invites light, concocted.

Respite seems a museum is January—
respite seems a museum is January.

My craving traces
and sorts out attitudinal shifts
until I decide.

Learn me, do remember me.

You arrive and we notice that her small placement rusts.

"Except if a report was filed."

"Sure," I say.

"See that seal? It invites touch, invites a display of insides."

"I sit with spirits."

January, a memorial, or scholarly—
January a memorial or scholarly.

Trucks took pieces of the ruin to the pier where we sat and ate lunch. Watching fear sent off in a barge, you said,

"You know, the memorial will feature a museum."

We shook our heads.

We walked on sidewalks washed down as a firm began its design.

Pulled out from my pocket, I show you "Sevastopol after liberation, May 1944," a photo by Yevgeny Khaldei. The bombed city is the background for five young people in bathing suits, sunning themselves on rocks near the sea. The perspective is from the sea.

I remember thinking that our ruin was beautiful and as the days grew shorter, the tall piece, like framing for a cathedral, was illuminated, steaming from the water used to cool the fires below.

"Others have said this. And photographs," you remind me.

Meanwhile, our tour guide wears a hooped skirt. "Note the gardens, the architecture, the furnishings, the artworks. The research to acquire the most likely chair, table, drapery."

"Are the furnishings original?"

"Yes. Most."

I notice the work to erase the slave quarters, oil refineries up the river, chemical plants barely visible through the trees. Her evacuated black skin and my admission ticket, white.

Moving in a group around carefully weeded pathways, flowers and cut shrubs at our ankles, our focus is on her lacy umbrella, diligently following her pointing, speech.

Because the string broke for me
therefore the place does not feel to me

as the place used to feel to me
on account of it

The place feels as if it stood open
because the string has broken for me

therefore the place does not feel pleasant
to me because of it

Uncertain how my body holds the memory, I have no visible scar.

Still, I move through the city, collecting groceries for the evening, or a morning newspaper for the discomfort of it.

There are those with a relic: black box ten inches high, an urn inside, of mahogany, wrapped in a dark purple drawstring sack of velvet.

There are those who walk the grassy pile an island away.

I have not drawn a line to that point.

So I cabinet, I barricade, I curate and slot the missing—
tracing labored breaths. But this could be from an existing condition
or if I have stepped on a piece of the clean up.

Over my left shoulder in the morning, right in the evening.

Everyone marveled how fast. Now some complain about how slow,
the museum, the memorial. Some never speak. Unraveled, I want slower.

At the Office, I unroll one of the blueprints:

In the first place, the changing gallery.
In the second, the Café, the Gift Shoppe. 10:46 am. Dusk.
Lively hub of orientation and ticketing. Resource Center. Midnight.

What is not in the plan:

"On day 2,531 of her vigil opposite the National Civil Rights Museum, (photo with kind permission of Jacqueline Smith) it is she—if we will look—who shocks us out of solemnity, promoting more than mourning, nostalgia, or paralysis."

Another set of instructions:

Go straight up the road that bisects the parking lot and take the footpath uphill from the old Buchenwald Bahnhof. Or take Strasse der Nationen to the end, forty minutes. Take a look at the pond whose banks are still murky with human ashes and bone fragments and every effort to present the facts. Note the sobering contrast to the charm of half-timber and heather.

Tip: In summer the tables spill out onto the street for a very Italian feeling.

Take a bike tour, castle admission not included, always confirming that your guide is officially qualified.

Tip:

Do it yourself.

How Societies Remember by Paul Connerton

"The Exhibitionary Complex" in *The Birth of the Museum: History, Theory, Politics* by Tony Bennett

"World Heritage and Cultural Economics" by Barbara Kirshenblatt-Gimblett in *Museum Frictions*

"Isn't This a Wonderful Place? (A Tour of the Tour of the Guggenhaim Bilbao)" by Andrea Fraser in *Museum Frictions*

"Local Color: The Southern Plantation in Popular Culture" by Jessica Adams in *Cultural Critique*

"Excursions into the Un-Remembered Past: What People Want from Visits to Historical Sites" by Catherine M. Cameron and John B. Gatewood in *The Public Historian*

I go looking for my mentor. I study the way she sighs, hangs her hands on the lapels of her uniform, surveys the growing crowd, slips on some comfortable shoes, and says:

"We'll call them Experience Stages. Documentary Zones. Semi-enclosed spaces. Parental guidance areas so that families, according to their children, may edit."

She begins to walk and continues:

"We'll call them contact zones, connective tissue. Quiet alcoves and simple benches. Interior and exterior gardens from which to escape: refuges."

"Refugees," I mutter.

We go on, walking together, though I am more apart.

"Windows as tiny slots reveal the outside pillars of this city, its marble colu. that are to be our angels. Everything is vertical."

"I'm not so sure about that," I interject.

She rips my stub sternly in response.

The phone on her belt rings and I take advantage of this distraction, gently pushing against the crash bar. I end up in an alley—

Later that night I go back. It is not clear whether I have broken in or used the front door. I say hello carefully and she asks, "Why attempt to draw water from stone and what could you desire in this country so designed?"

My answer:

"Here is what to see or frenzy. I am measured against this flag."

We are bewildered at this exchange even though I've sounded convincing.

She tries to get us back on track, asking, "Why use poetry? Is this?"

I clear my voice and make a compartment from the space between my hands:

"I notice more colors in September and people's faces. Who was here, before. For example, I don't mind winter now that August has changed for me. Slower, and my loved ones and friends, I want to ask them."

She nods.

For example, he said, "Please no more memorials." It was called, "Take Back the Memorial." She said, "Please, just nothing below ground." He said, "I've turned my back on those sixteen acres." She wrote, "Fix it, please. Show these people the door." She said, "For months she would not say a word, and would always look at the floor," adding, "and others told me of the sight of people and paper in the air."

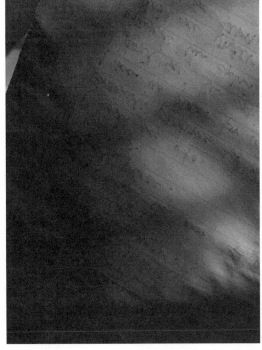

I awake to find my neighbor at the door, with one candle lit, and a second one, unlit, for me.

"Come."

It is simple, our feeling. I follow her down to the lobby to find many others there, mostly quiet, some weeping. I feel tender even toward the ones with different politics who complain about the heat on the sixth floor and all the ethnicities.

I clutch a piece of paper with my left hand. These are not our instructions:

The visitors are the forgiving party.
The men and the women sit down and weep together.
The dancers shake their enemies from the back.
This is the squelching song.

The next day, I am back at work, feeling inspired and tender, and find that they have distributed this, from the Office:

"This is the street-level expanse with groves of white oaks and where sweet gum trees will rise around two voids bordered by names and filled with waterfalls and pools."

This is a perfect example of street-level belief.
It has never been clear where I should walk.

They turned off the bridge lights. Gone, our starry drape.
We watched a monarch butterfly try to migrate across the narrows,
surprised to feel glad to see a battleship anchored there.

Am I turning to poetry? As an escape or to make sense?

Meanwhile, daily, we see each other to the door and I watch until you turn the corner.

Later, my bad dreams go largely unmentioned at the Office, in museums, or around the conference table. Back behind our door, candles are lit and we sometimes speak about this:

to wince at the sight of a fellow creature's skin infringed.

I decline. I cabinet and so barricaded, I remain, reading,

"African-American visitors reported that they felt discomfort in their bones, lightheadedness, heavy heart." Listening, you say, "Makes sense to me."

For my notebook:

Bad policies may be felt experiences.

Someone walked off with our federal government.

But there was rarely protection, historically. Or for some.

Two months later, around the table, he shouted, "No, I won't be quiet!"

It was supposed to be a holiday. I wanted to speak about my event, but he insisted on history and for a year I was angry, even though I understood "Rosewood" "my people" "original terror."

Survey:

Did you know that the attack on Rosewood was planned and publicized?

Stutter:

A desire for comparison. Read "companion."

his brother went away after working the ferry
that for months took families down to gather

the lilies   *his brother lived the sentences*
the lilies to gather   *this brother*

who went with families
down to where no one wanted

went away after working the ferry
that for months took families down to gather

In November, a place loosened in my throat, I got rid of it, and thought I was sick like the others.

"Perhaps the voids now define a design line that cannot be crossed."

Thinking that dispatches such as the above were taking a toll on my body, I sought out the following:

"Violent city: resembling an ink spot splashed onto the sky—

we saw, together, the glass towers slip and the light quiver shut.

Violent forest: stitched together in wet tunnels."

Dear Theater:

By climbing aboard the actual bus on which Rosa Parks' protest began, we can sit down and become the subject to a recording of the driver's voice demanding that we, positioned as Rosa Parks, move or leave.

Dear Tower of Hope:

A glass elevator takes visitors down to a meditation garden in which an artistically rendered calendar stone marks all the days of communal memorial where visitors can leave flowers and tokens of remembrance.

Hall of Commitment:

Here they sign a statement of personal commitment to the cause, their portrait is taken, and their faces are added to a video-mosaic of faces that merge and rise up the tower in an iconic representation of the community of Human Rights constantly replenishing itself.

Dear Observatory:

The global perspective through evidentiary video and reports from—

Map: my sites of conscience clean—

To-do List: and how you can join, can make

This: the practical, participate

Activist: part of the museum that makes it possible for visitors to:

walk out with a concrete to-do list they can call up on their computers at home or print out as they leave and—

Bridge: between each level visitors watch each other

Return: to the bridges, which house hundreds, perhaps eventually thousands of faces:

stories and interviews with people who have resisted oppression
in clean images:

in clean images constantly replenishing:

cascading down the ramp and will include notable figures

along with me, constantly replenishing,

Sincerely, clean—

track the wolf through the marble
and gather the absence   track

the wolf swiftly   swiftly we secularized
where ashes came down to gather

carry them swiftly   the sentences and
track the wolf through the marble

carry us down to suffer
the lilies   the limits of you but to listen

swiftly we sacrilized the marble the lilies
the limits of images   to track

Dear J.,

Meet me at the mansion unbuilt,

at the romance of the ruin or the infrastructure raw,

at the rudely interrupted slave quarters converted into restrooms.

I will walk across bare boards,

and meet you at the childbirthing couch, where we are encouraged to fill the empty areas and people them with the family we learned of, leaving a gap wherein primarily white tourists can insert this brochure.

Barricade
Wince-net

Barb
Brochure

Razor
Tour

and Caption.

The Devil's Rope Museum, the Spilger Barbed Wire Collection.
To pass through, you must fold your arms.

Haunted by the image of skin grazing metal, I hesitate before pressing send.

Subject line:
"How did you come to this?"

Reply:
"Then came all of the complications about 'whose disaster was it?' and why should I lament my city while violence happens all over and every day. But I had lost faith in this body even if previously I had been critical of the violence that lead to The Office, the attacks."

"Our official attacks?" she mishears. I attempt to change the subject:

"Forensic evidence points to the fact that the African Burial Ground bodies were worked to death."

"I like that word 'forensic.'" she responds.

Finally, with her fingertips she has closed my eyes.

Dear Floor Plan:

These three photographs that depict the torture and hanging of Frank Embree were laced together with a twisted purple thread, so as to unfold like a map.

Dear Palette:

And those of us who came to look at fascinating distortions of steel have now been silenced by that tiny figure—

Dear Fascinator:

The museum will be an exemplar of accessibility; it will speak different languages; it will provide access to our stories through a diverse palette of multimedia techniques.

Dear Seeker:

Far more affecting are the unaltered electric fences and blown-up gas chambers. Tip: You may camp nearby from April to October.

Meanwhile, I watch the blacksmith bang out a nail, horseshoes, or handcuffs and chains. At the Colonial Williamsburg Escaped Slave Program, begun in 2000, guests are approached by a runaway slave. Visitors know that they are surrounded by slave catchers and so the park's guests must react instinctively to the situation. "This has turned out to be a really intense visitor experience and is one of its most popular programs."

"Or the Polynesian Cultural Center, a Mormon operation where, since 1963, Mormon students at Brigham Young University Hawaii keep alive and share their island heritage with visitors while working their way through school."

Meanwhile, "the Gurwani community was forced to relocate to make way for an open-air museum. When they resisted, force was used, including bulldozers and armed police, resulting in four deaths and many injuries."

The next day, I mail the following letter:

Dear Survey:
More than a structure, what do you feel? More than a sentence.

Dream that I stood in a cornfield, but was the corn cut or growing?
How has your breathing been? How far beneath and silently?

Wanting time to insert interpretation into the event,
I remain, as object of their looking, Sincerely,

She writes back: "But were you there?"

It is "here," trapped between the photographs. Meanwhile, I have only you to
tell, and there is limited access to the box beam remnants.

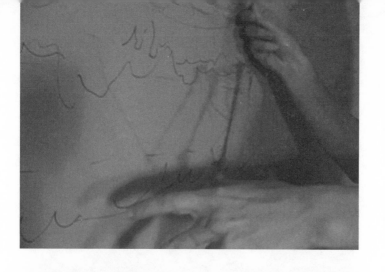

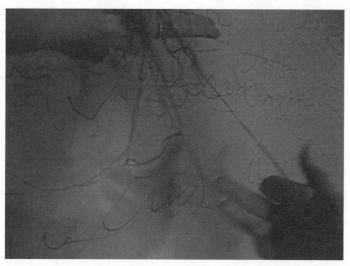

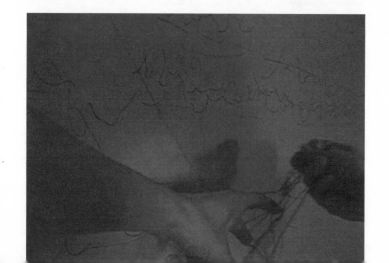

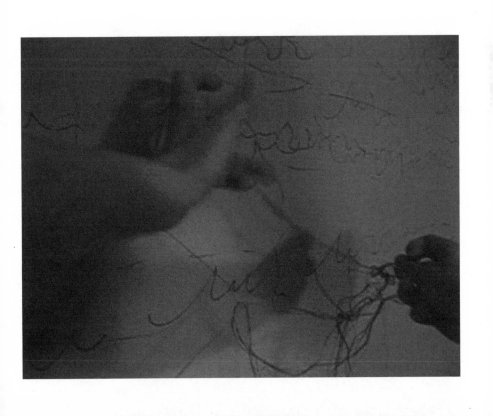

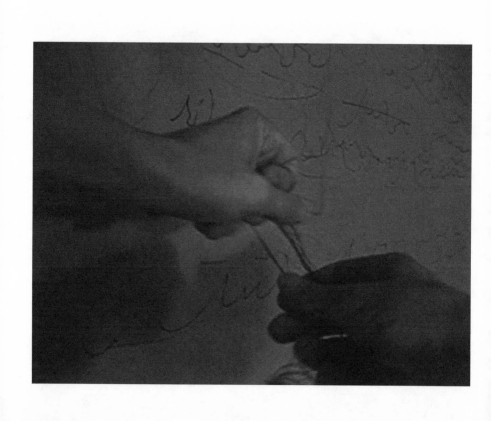

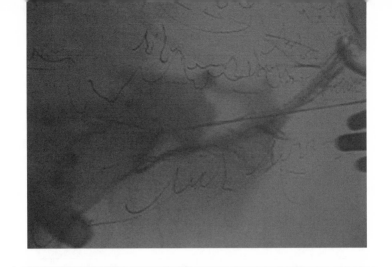

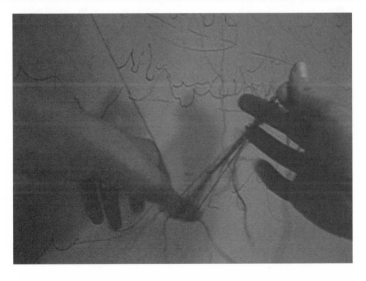

Let's Go Germany

Frommer's Germany 2007

Fodor's Germany 2008

Fodor's Eastern and Central Europe 2007

"Slavery in New York" exhibit brochure, New York Historical Society

"The String Game" by Dia!Kwain, "Peacemaking event" from the Andaman Islands, "Grease Feast Event" and "Gift Event" from the Kwakiutl Indians, "Forest Event" from Hungary collected in *Technicians of the Sacred* edited by Jerome Rothenberg

"Fragments from a History of Ruin" by Brian Dillon in *Cabinet*

when the impulse is to go away   to bury
I wade through the deep muddy

when the impulse is to pass behind a cloud
hide   I wade through the deep and muddy

when   come a drummer
come a-beating drum

when I feel the darkness deeply
twist in me like a river

to the hollow of my hands
to my city of sleepers   come a drummer

come a beating drum   I'm wading
through the deep muddy

fool says push on
fool says push on

Dear J.,
Disappointment at the pit forms around a poster of ruins.

They read maps of now everyone's place, unfit for the lens through chain link, or to smile in the foreground.

What seeps as a platform tickets: pity, a narrative.

On the way to work, they tap me on the shoulder and I help point downtown, advertised as available space, help pull complexity from charms and T-shirts to be worn out.

Later, the gradually winding and ramped hallway gently shows us how to go. Glass railings, skylights above, all heighten our sense of sight. Nothing is too differentiated as to shock as the space draws us forward, upward, toward a feeling that we are the mapmakers who know the vocabulary of knowledge, of fashion, how to live.

White is the dominant color, or lack, signaling availability, the new.

We feel close to our companions—we may even be on a date. If alone, I am even more softened, emptied out, a little lonely, and this feeling makes my desire to learn more intense.

There is a culminating gift shop.

Dear Guest Book:

"After all, we could feel, hear the heartbeat."

"Entrancing, a little sad."

"Wonderful exhibit. Clear. Left with a sense of peacefulness."

"Thank you for sharing."

"Bought the book."

In the elevator, a recording of a soldier's voice describes the scene and concludes by asking:

"How could it happen?"

Purchase a guidebook. Walk through the notorious gate.

I said I would go to where the people have dreams, right at dawn.

(The soft gauze of new light on this subject matter.)

Going to Cortlandt Street to pray. (You don't pray.)

I am going to that town. Going over the Atlantic to pray. To Promised Land School (but you hear "Thomasland") to pray.

Let me go.
Let me see you, friends with nightmares.
Let me go.
Let me see you, friends with remember, friends with pray.

Field of sunlight. (Dark cloud.)

Soft marsh grasses. (Soaking of cracked hands.)

It is the time of the crocus thaw. Remnants surge out of the ground.

Do you want to see?

Come into this night with me, for I am not a good sufferer.

Don't shore your light up on my sea. I want you cracked.

That night I dream of archaeological evidence behind a scrim.
Tiny pins with labels attached appear enlarged as flags.
Limb, tooth, socket, injustice.

I awake knowing that everything is proof. I don't tell you this right away.

Two days later, you say, "I don't like this, your keeping things from me."
You light candles and sleep.

Meanwhile, I move along the stainless steel lab tables, looking.

Next to his picture, she has written, "I was given Mr. Galvin's name and I will be praying for him and his family for many years to come."

Later, for my notebook:
Because within the borders of my body I feel unable to discuss this good freedom, these exhibits.

She answers:
I wonder if we have become too weak to stand up to the scrutiny at the edge of the abyss.

But who is this we?
When was this become?
And which freedom? Which abyss?

Survey:

Is there anything that makes an historical site particularly enjoyable for you?

Shh.

Hmm.

Them.

I'd prefer not to please follow me.

On the Natural History of Destruction and *Austerlitz* by W. G. Sebald

By the Bias of Sound by Gustaf Sobin

"Collections of Confinement: Thoughts on Barbed Wire" by Reviel Netz in *Connect*

Web site of The Human Rights Museum

The 9/11 Memorial Process Team Briefing Book edited by Johannah Rodgers

"On Looking: Lynching Photographs and Legacies of Lynching after 9/11" by Dora Apel in *American Quarterly*

"Culture and Constraints: Further Thoughts on Ethnography and Exhibiting" by Henrietta Lidchi in *International Journal of Heritage Studies*

"Angels in the Temple: the Aesthetic Construction of Citizenship at the United States Holocaust Memorial Museum" by Greig Crysler and Abidin Kusno in *Art Journal*

then I had news   people were washed away they say
water went away they say   fog was not complete

they say your eyes do not make mistakes
people were washed away

from the nothing
the increase

from the tile the paver the sacred the numinous
to gather from his hairbrush the news

the fork the wire the sacred small papers of rain
the beam the cutter was not they say

from the nothing
the increase the many the faded the washed away

your eyes do not make mistakes
they say

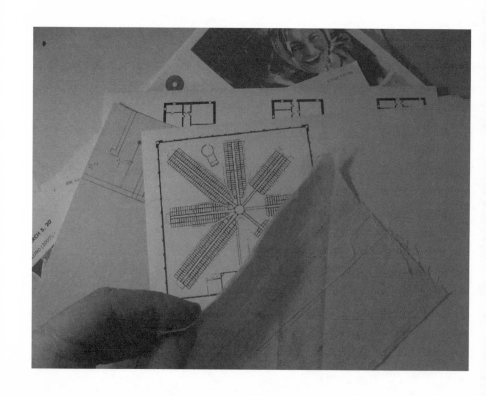

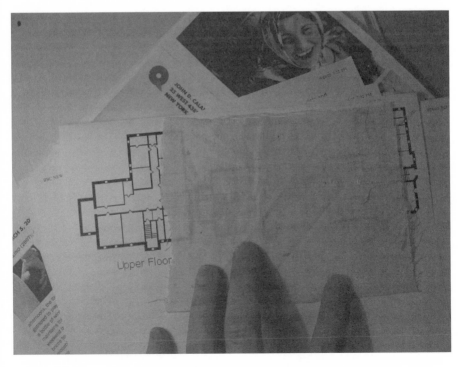

"On my way to Hiroshima," wrote Noguchi, "where I was to propose the design of two bridges for the Peace Park, I stopped by the city of Gifu to watch the cormorant fishing."

How far beneath and silently?

"A low wall, perhaps four feet in height, surrounds upturned video monitors emitting blue light. This modesty screen is intended to prevent small children from watching the graphic and murderous scenes."

"A clerestory, pronounced clearstory, is a high wall with a band of narrow windows along the very top."

She wrote that disasters are revealers.

Which comfort do you seek, wringing out the sorrow previously held
in order to make way for the new?

How much violence is an echo?

I await your reply, which I expect will be global—

Dear Flannel-board Story Activity:

Please help students compare their lives to the enslaved child.

Dear Charter of Rights and Freedoms: Welcome

to a dynamic opinion pulse

that illustrates the tensions of translating. Dear Lesson Plan:

watch digitally enlarged sentences scroll upward in a vertical polling chamber
and feel the proof of it,

my craning neck. Dear Conspiracy: Take your opinion

and make me a city.

Dear Tower of Faces: I know nothing about you

except your collective status as victim. Archive: We are coping

with huge sets of historical data.

Visitors: Use your key

to record opinions immediately,

tally and present your pillar of thought, your architect, our father, your mark.

Sincerely yours, White Wall of Rescuers.

On the lowest right corner of the wall, I read the following instructions:

To see the real thing, no reconstructions, a student will make a diorama depicting history to the left, such as Anne Frank, and to the right of the register: black people in miniature, plus a squaw, another squaw,

to purchase
to make a disaster event
with feathers with beads with real—

We tell the world what the children draw for sale will save us.

Dear Venn Diagram:
Students will write a class story dealing with a slave who becomes free, using free-writing to express feelings, fast, without thinking, without crossing out, and preferably timed.

"Platforms will be built with seminal views to reconnect the visitor to the outside world."

But visitor, where did you go?

A marble floor tile shifts

and in its loosened state I slip down into a basement
where I meet Fred Wilson, mining the museum, saying:

"This situation in the world is not particularly worse than other moments. It just depends on who you are. It helps to diffuse the anxiety knowing that you're in this continuum."

He pulls paintings out of storage. He draws a line to that point.

"Despite red velvet linings, memories are like nettles that come back long after the first touch."

"Whose memories?"

"I have a family," answers the didactic.

from the nothing the increase
I make a space

between me and this room
what I feel of my old sadness

is a shining blue-like body
from the nothing to the increase

I reproduce myself endlessly
causing little figures

drawing thin lines
I break

with mourning
after the 13th day

Rough Guide to the USA

Let's Go USA

Rough Guide to New York City

Regarding the Pain of Others by Susan Sontag

Lonely Planet USA

The Language of Inquiry and *One Continuous Mistake* hold bookmarks that read "Borders Books."

A month after the event, the kind man told me to go and mourn the destroyed books. He unfurled the following blueprint:

To give a glass bowl.
Go into the forest and hang their clothes from trees.

To make a new entrance to the building.
Give everyone a new name.

So as to remember the ruin
leave a space in the new house undone—

Meanwhile, Peter Eisenman explains how he fought to keep names off the stones of the Berlin Holocaust memorial.

At the ceremony to mark the beginning of its construction, he stumbles: "I never at many moments thought we would build this and here it is."

The project is delayed when the company commissioned to make an anti-graffiti coating for the stones is found to have also produced gas for Nazi extermination camps.

On the day that the memorial opens, an "unidentified youth" is photographed jumping from pillar to pillar.

Dear Documentary:
Catalogue this wood-rot, this moss
encroaching. Preserve the footprint.
Bar-code a furrowed brow.

Please slot
your next erosion event with us.

"Berlin Builds Holocaust Memorial" by Barbara Miller, BBC News Berlin, December 15, 2004

"Berlin's Holocaust Memorial Opens to Public" by Emily Harris, NPR, May 12, 2005

"Berlin Opens Holocaust Memorial" BBC News, May 10, 2005

"Performing the Real Thing in the Postmodern Museum" by Tracy C. Davis in *The Drama Review*

"On the Uses of Relativism: Fact, Conjecture, and Black and White Histories at Colonial Williamsburg," by Eric Gable, Richard Handler, Anna Lawson in *American Ethnologist*

"To Be a Slave" and "Lifting the Veil," curriculum guides from the Booker T. Washington National Historic Site

"My Dear H." by Ingeborg Drewitz, translated by Gerrit Jackson in *Connect*

the people went down to look
his brother went   our sister

went down to look for lilies   took the ferry
that went   to carry

me down to look for that place
on account of it   his brother wrote

the sentences and gathered the lilies
and the ground and the string broke for him

so he went away on account of it
from looking from gathering

A proclaim here sits.

All have learned monuments to ancestors who never confess.

Marble veins the value
from which forgiveness shrinks.

Which self-monitoring portable wall,
which lenient spur-wheels gouge,
which nerves just below?
Vicious (smaller and more painful)
or obvious (less pain but larger)?

There is no answer to the technology of the fence.

Cut a piece and carry it with you and you are now the one who grows.

"Who knows?" I mishear.

Dear J.,
Why would you be shocked by the violence of that day?

Clipboard in hand, I inventory the titles received:

The Listening Lost,
Heart on a Tripod,
Night Season,
Surface Tension: a 10 Day Tryst,
The Ridiculous Concept of Smiling.

Each envelope, a rip open, reading:

The Shadows of Ideas,
Chambers for a Memory Palace,
Method of Loci,
My Home Is Over Jordan.
Or where the bundles of ancestors were placed,
between language and violence—

"Various cultures conceive of hostile behavior as aberrant and anti-social and thus miss what is common and everyday about violence."

Possible title:

Everyday Violence.

"Insecurity by Design" by Mark Wigley in *After the World Trade Center: Rethinking New York City*

Befallen I by Erin Moure

"Whose Downtown?!?" by John Kuo Wei Tchen in *After the World Trade Center: Rethinking New York City*

"So Much Trouble in the World – Believe it or Not!" an installation by Fred Wilson at the Hood Museum, Dartmouth College

"Waist Deep in the Big Muddy" as sung by Pete Seeger

The Isamu Noguchi Garden Museum with text by Isamu Noguchi

"Slavery in New York" exhibit brochure, the New York Historical Society

It is now another spring and I wait, sitting on the edge of a folding chair in a wide hallway near the main entrance. I think through the theories,

such as speech and throne, deciding
that a father must be read backwards. (For he is not a good sufferer.)

I watch mothers behind sheer curtains
privately cataloguing

securing folds
against the fluorescent hum of the grid.

Meanwhile, another crocus thaw. Come more remnants up out of our ground. The mothers already know.

A nurse interrupts my waiting. "Too much thinking!" she declares, walking purposefully toward me, extending her hand—

"Hello Architect: Do you want to see?"

"That's not me," I reply.

Her fingers press and pull me anyway.

Meanwhile, all student ticketholders will write a paragraph

about what freedom means, or a return to gracious living at Madewood,
at Laura, softly hooped.

"Praline for me a recipe!" someone shouts, piercing the historical quiet.

The guide brags about the recipe's numinous effects.

There are art servants. Event planters.
Some have fallen south, or toward the coal north.

There is the necessary butler
and heroes list and lean on the nursemaid.
Her working displays: How are they alike?
How are they different?

Sliding a hand over the wall, seeing where it might give.
When she isn't looking,

I push and slip inside a drawer.

Earlier that year,

I wore a mask to work.

Four years later, bones were found in the bank.
I can't decide if this is hopeful.

Forensic Archeology Recovery creates the acronym FAR.
I remember how much she liked that word.

Four weeks later, in one of the upstairs galleries filled with Noguchi's paper lights, I see a man with a white bandage wrapped around his head.

Daily, he receives faxes picturing the damage and documenting the progress in shoring it up.

Two weeks later they clean up Union Square, and visitors fall in love with the heart of Warsaw, restored.

The important thing was for the slurry wall to hold. Dear Committee to Save:

Do not weep for this missing cultural heritage site. Do not weep for this missing. Insert possible titles here:

Such as Niche, Slot, or the plural of niche.

Notch, Slit.

"The state will provide for the destruction of some sites. The state builds and destroys." This sounds too biblical.

"The poetics of the exhibition, destruction." Too academic.

"I call it Destroy." This is a quote from Penelope.

"Some rooms cannot be destroyed, such as quilt or a veil that tosses itself over camera."

"Some rooms should not be inhabited." This is a favorite.
Finally, we agree.

At dawn I feel the loss of that oncoming day.

3 pm. 5:51. 6:30. Who is not coming home.

Around the dinner table, with your hand you make a gentle chopping motion in the air off to the side of your face. "Global politics and this current war," you say, "are backdrops to my depression."

when the impulse is to go away
to bury

to pass behind a cloud
to hide and secret

come a drummer
come a-beating drum

when you feel the darkness
twist in you like a river

to the hollow of your hands
to your city of sleepers

come a drummer
come a-beating drum

"Build the Memorial First" editorial, *The New York Times*, March 10, 2006

"Memorial Cost at Ground Zero Nears $1 Billion" by Charles V. Bagli and David W. Dunlap, *The New York Times*, May 5, 2006

"The 500 Hours of 9/11" by Glenn Collins, *The New York Times*, May 30, 2006

"Cai Guo-Qiang on the Roof: Transparent Monument" exhibit brochure, the Metropolitan Museum of Art

"Air Masks at Issue in Claims of 9/11 Illnesses" by Anthony DePalma, *The New York Times*, June 5, 2006

Rachel Whiteread by Charlotte Mullins

"Ralph Lemon Explores Southern Pain through Dance" by William Loeffler, *The Pittsburg Tribune-Review*, March 17, 2005

"Sculpture crashes to floor in NY museum" Australian Broadcast Corporation, July 2, 2008

Dear Gesture Technology:
there is something called "gesture technology."

Dear Privately:
the AIDS quilt, the Mothers of the Plaza del Mayo, homemade posters
of the missing. Tape. String. Snapshots. He requested,

"Please, no more memorials."

Sir,

Table,

Barricade,

Note the crack that cuts through the figures of Valor, Victory, and Peace.

Dear "Slowly Slowly,"

Dear Night, further dematerialized. I am—

Vestibule:

where I collect
scant accumulations of voice. Marble:

where I shed this axiology
and open wide.

Hinge:

Onlooker:

a sharp memorial grids. Gallery: versus our body's fluid floor plan

versus a freedom feeling
and twenty-nine lynching photos
on three walls
framed in light Georgia oak.
Further frames:

Rubber plinth.
Twenty-five spaces.
Black bath.

Untitled (library).
Untitled (basement).
Untitled (one hundred spaces).

Water tower.
Table and chair (clear).
Untitled (slab).

Cell. False door. A monument
feeling—

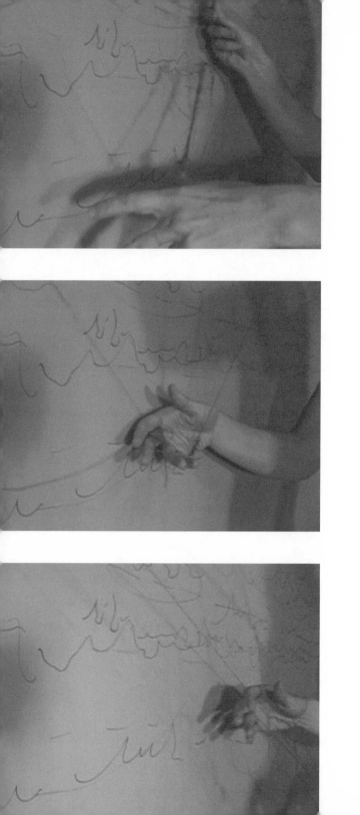

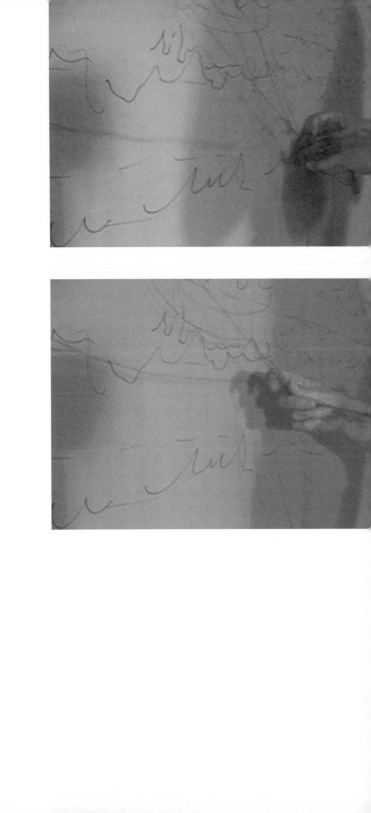

Unfold the storm keys.

Read new columns held damply.

And bones, their bones, the clean of it, gone.

What walls and wills deliver or cut? Answer:
Four weeks. Five years. Minutes after.
Still, each time I go back to the site,

I dream of a huge aboveground tomb whose stone door glides back and forth, obstructing my view of half the city. The white marble glows brightly and threatens to blind me completely. I think to take a photograph.

My mentor again appears, asking, "Have you seen the library inside out?"

Before I can respond, Rachel Whiteread steps out of the shadows and explains:

"I knew my piece was going to be a memorial, and I wasn't quite sure if it would be respected. So I made replaceable book pieces that are bolted from the inside, and a series of extra pieces to serve as replacements if necessary, in case there is some terrible graffiti."

I wake up and collect the following:

He was on the train that goes over the bridge and saw.
She was below, in the lobby.
I was in front of.
They were up 6th Avenue looking at.
He made the mistake of

while she was there buying.

He went to the bridge and saw.

Covered in. "She had lost."

"Their eyes looking." "I wanted." "To my knees."

track the wolf
through the marble

track the wolf through acres
track the wolf through the hole

in the fencing   track the wolf
through the images   from the nothing

the increase the wolf
through the foyer the files the archive

to track

Wrenched from the tendency to ignore, I want memory wrenched from the tendency to protest,

from the ruin of argument, saying,

"Come crowd yourself with me in rooms of the ruin."

Because if I flee consolation

if I midnight. If I contest claims to store, stock, arcade,
exhibit, slot—

If a frame
made from the body
is broken and vulnerable to vines,

then everything is touched with names, everything touched with engrave,

everything touched with scar, art, touched with slavery, a profit is touched with generous support, a museum basement, stairs, name and hope,

the everything of video, push to play, everything within the knit of the city touched down by wooden planks, steel, unloading,

is everyone touched down by disaster, iron, translation on display, the everything touched by reasonable,

touched with the lures of words,

every one touched the rope and broke, the world is whole, touched
by the sloop, the wind,

an arrival hunts down an idea, a body, to exhibit

is nothing not touched with generous support, is nothing bound
by the book, carefully a record engraved or in flames

while the world is made by debris, around a table, the cast-off grows,
the cinders—

ACKNOWLEDGMENTS

Portions of this manuscript, in somewhat different forms, have appeared in *Boog City*, *Effing Journal*, *Miniature Forests*, and *Action, Yes*. Thanks to those editors for their support. Work on *SLOT* began during a Lower Manhattan Cultural Council residency in 2006-2007; I want to thank the entire LMCC staff for the time and space to create.

Language on pages 13, 26, 37, 53, 67, 79, 83, 89, 109, and 121 can be traced back to the following works: "The String Game" by Dia!kwain, "Peacemaking event" from the Andaman Islands, "Grease Feast Event" and "Gift Event" from the Kwakiutl Indians, and "Forest Event" from Hungary, all collected in *Technicians of the Sacred*, edited by Jerome Rothenberg. Language on page 53 is also from "Waist Deep in the Big Muddy" by Pete Seeger. Some titles on page 92 are from the chapbooks of a Dusie Kollectiv exchange. Language on page 115 is from the titles of Rachel Whiteread's sculptures. Elsewhere, I have incorporated lines and phrases from the bibliographic citations that run through the book. This "incorporation" is a result of reading and research, writing and rewriting. It is my hope that *SLOT* may be a conduit back to these texts, an invitation to study and make brand new incorporations.

Thanks to to Sara Jordenö and Nanna Debois Buhl for their help editing and placing the images. Thanks to Evelyn Reilly, Jennifer Firestone, Stephen Motika, Joanna Sondheim, Ellen Baxt, Tisa Bryant, Karen Garthe, and Jonny Farrow for their feedback on the text.

SLOT is for New York City: its people and ghosts.

Jill Magi's projects combine research with the following forms: poetry, fiction, the essay, drawing, photography, and embroidery. She is the author of *Cadastral Map* (Shearsman), *Torchwood* (Shearsman), *Threads* (Futurepoem), as well as the chapbooks *Die for love, furlough* (In Edit Mode), *Poetry Barn Barn!* (2nd Avenue), *Cadastral Map* (Portable Press at Yo-Yo Labs), and numerous small, handmade books. In 2011, she was an artist-in-residence at the Textile Arts Center in Brooklyn, New York, and was a writer-in-residence with Lower Manhattan Cultural Council in 2006-07. Her visual works have been exhibited at the Textile Arts Center, the Brooklyn Arts Council Gallery, apexart, AC Institute Gallery, and Pace University. Jill runs Sona Books, a chapbook press, and teaches at Goddard College.

This book was published in an edition of 1,000 copies. It was printed and bound by McNaughton & Gunn in Saline, Michigan, using covers printed at Printing Gallery in New York City. It was designed and typeset by goodutopian using Centaur and Universe.

Ugly Duckling Presse is a nonprofit publishing collective based in Brooklyn. *SLOT* is the fourteenth title in UDP's Dossier Series, which was founded in 2008 to highlight works of an investigative nature presented in diverse forms: poetry, essay, criticism, interview, artist book, polemical text. For more on UDP or the Dossier Series, please visit us on the Web.

www.uglyducklingpresse.org